Where's the water?

THE WATER CYCLE

By Barbara M. Linde

 Gareth Stevens
PUBLISHING

Please visit our website, www.garethstevens.com. For a free color catalog of all our high-quality books, call toll free 1-800-542-2595 or fax 1-877-542-2596.

Library of Congress Cataloging-in-Publication Data

Names: Linde, Barbara M., author.
Title: The water cycle / Barbara M. Linde.
Description: New York : Gareth Stevens Publishing, [2016] | Series:
   Where's the water? | Includes bibliographical references and index.
Identifiers: LCCN 2016009791 | ISBN 9781482446883 (pbk.) | ISBN 9781482446906 (library bound) | ISBN 9781482446890 (6 pack)
Subjects: LCSH: Hydrologic cycle–Juvenile literature. |
   Water-supply–Juvenile literature.
Classification: LCC GB662.3 .L558 2016 | DDC 551.48–dc23
LC record available at http://lccn.loc.gov/2016009791

First Edition

Published in 2017 by
Gareth Stevens Publishing
111 East 14th Street, Suite 349
New York, NY 10003

Designer: Katelyn E. Reynolds
Editor: Kristen Nelson

Photo credits: Cover, p. 1 ShaunWilkinson/Shutterstock.com; cover, pp. 1–24 (background) vitalez/
Shutterstock.com; pp. 4–21 (circle splash) StudioSmart/Shutterstock.com; p. 5 DUSAN ZIDAR/
Shutterstock.com; p. 7 MARK GARLICK/SCIENCE PHOTO LIBRARY/Getty Images; p. 9 courtesy of NASA;
p. 11 jopelka/Shutterstock.com; p. 13 Jon Bilous/Shutterstock.com; p. 15 Vladimir Melnikov/Shutterstock.com;
p. 17 (inset) Adam Gryko/Shutterstock.com; p. 17 (main) bikeriderlondon/Shutterstock.com; p. 18 ekler/
Shutterstock.com; p. 19 Anton_Ivanov/Shutterstock.com; p. 21 Kazakova Maryia/Shutterstock.com.

Printed in the United States of America

CPSIA compliance information: Batch #CS16GS. For further information, contact Gareth Stevens, New York, New York at 1-800-542-2595.

CONTENTS

Words in the glossary appear in **bold** type
the first time they are used in the text.

DROP BY DROP

Think of all the places you might find water. There's some in a **puddle** on the sidewalk. There's more in lakes, rivers, and small streams. A lot of water is in the ocean. You've seen rain falling from the sky. Perhaps you've played in the snow or seen hailstones.

Where does this water come from? And where does it go if it dries up? You'll learn the answers to these questions as you read all about the water cycle.

facts on Tap

A cycle is a set of events that happen the same way over and over again.

4

Water is a big part of our lives. We drink water and use it to wash and cook, too!

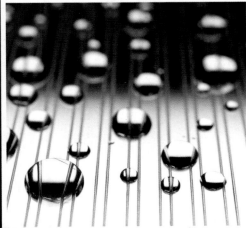

5

HOW DID WATER GET HERE?

Water is everywhere, but how did it get here in the first place? No one knows for sure. But scientists are looking for the answer.

One group of scientists announced a new **theory** in 2014. They were studying very old **meteorites**. The meteorites were found to have a makeup much like that of ancient rocks found on Earth, meaning they probably formed at the same time. The meteorites had a lot of water in them. This made the scientists think Earth had water from the start.

Facts on Tap

All living things need water to stay alive. A person can only live for about 3 days without water.

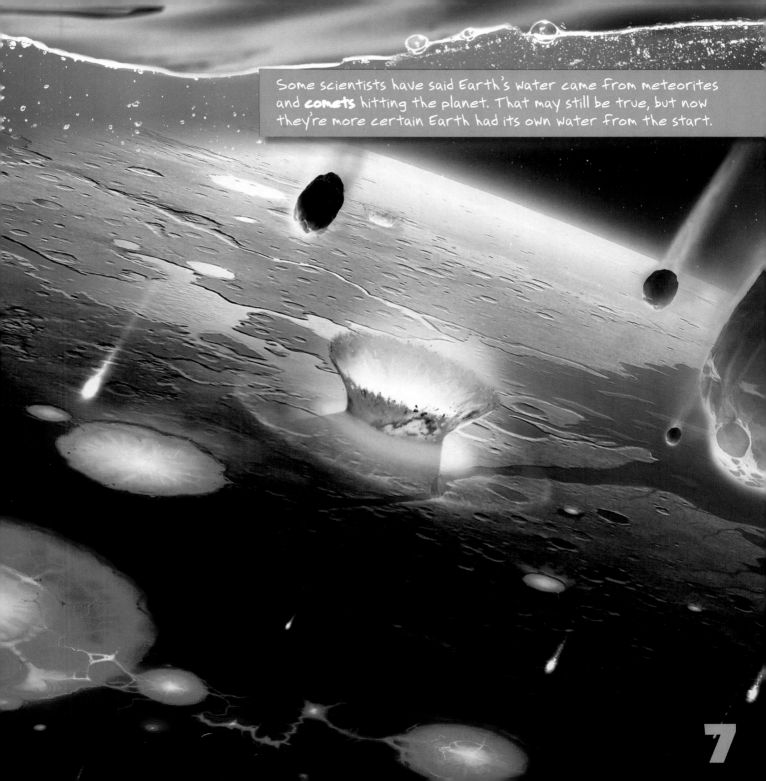

Some scientists have said Earth's water came from meteorites and **comets** hitting the planet. That may still be true, but now they're more certain Earth had its own water from the start.

THE THREE STATES OF WATER

Water covers about 75 percent, or three-fourths, of Earth. It's found in three different states, or forms. It's in liquid form in bodies of water all over the world, including oceans, lakes, rivers, and streams. Liquid water flows underground, too. This is called groundwater.

When water is frozen, it's a solid. Snow, glaciers, and ice caps are all forms of solid water. Some water exists as a gas in water vapor. You can't see it, but it's there.

Facts on Tap

In all, Earth has about 333 million cubic miles (1.4 billion cubic km) of water. Most of it is salt water in the oceans. The rest is freshwater.

When astronauts on *Apollo 17* first saw Earth from space, they called it the "big blue marble" because of all the water.

9

WHAT IS THE WATER CYCLE?

Earth has a set amount of water. It's been moving around on the ground, underground, and in the sky for billions of years. In fact, it's been moving around the planet since Earth formed! The "water cycle" is the name scientists give to this movement.

Because it's a cycle, there's no set beginning or end to water's movement. But there are three main parts of the water cycle: evaporation, condensation, and **precipitation**. Read on to learn how these are part of the cycle!

The water cycle never stops! It even moves water around the world.

EVAPORATION

Evaporation takes place when water **molecules** warm up. They then change from a liquid to a gas—water vapor. The water vapor rises into the air, or **atmosphere**.

Most evaporation takes place over oceans because they're the largest bodies of water. Water also evaporates from lakes, rivers, and wet ground. Liquid water also becomes a gas during plant **transpiration**. Ice can melt into liquid water and then evaporate. Sometimes, ice evaporates without changing to liquid water first! This is called sublimation.

facts on Tap

The water cycle is also called the hydrologic cycle. The word "hydrologic" comes from the roots hydr, meaning "water", and logos, meaning "knowledge of."

After it evaporates, a water molecule stays in the atmosphere for about 10 days.

13

CONDENSATION

The higher water vapor rises above Earth, the colder the air gets. The colder air cools the water vapor and changes it back into tiny liquid water droplets. The change of water from a gas to a liquid is called condensation.

Water droplets clump together to form a cloud. The droplets keep getting cooler. The cloud grows larger as more droplets join the others. When a cloud gets heavy enough, the next part of the water cycle begins.

Facts on Tap

Condensation doesn't just happen high up in the air. Fog is condensation close to Earth's surface.

Clouds might look light and fluffy, but they can be really heavy. A cloud can weigh as much as a jet!

15

PRECIPITATION

Some of the water in the clouds falls to Earth as precipitation. Rain is made of tiny droplets of liquid water. When the temperature in the cloud is below freezing, which is 32°F (0°C), water vapor condenses into ice **crystals**. The ice crystals join together to form snowflakes.

Sleet is rain that freezes as it falls. Freezing rain falls as liquid, but freezes when it reaches the ground. Hailstones are balls of ice that may fall during a thunderstorm.

facts on Tap

From August 1850 to July 1861, Cherrapunji, India, had more than 1,000 inches (2,540 cm) of rain. That's the most in a year ever recorded, anywhere!

16

Precipitation collects on land and water, and the water cycle starts again! Most precipitation falls as rain.

snow

STORING THE WATER

Some of Earth's water is always part of the water cycle. The rest is stored, or stays in the same state for a long time. A lot of water exists as ice in Antarctica and Greenland. Sometimes, big pieces of ice called icebergs break away. When they reach warm water, they melt.

Water is stored underground after it soaks into soil during rainstorms or as snow melts. People often dig wells to get this groundwater. They drink it and water crops with it.

Greenland

Antarctica

About 90 percent of the ice on Earth is in Antarctica.

EXPERIMENT WITH EVAPORATION

Here's an experiment you can do to watch evaporation in action. Start in the morning, outside. Pour the same amount of water in two small, clear plastic dishes. Mark a line at the top of the water. Put one dish in the sun and one in the shade. Check them about every hour. Draw or take pictures, and mark the water level.

What happens? The heat of the sun makes water molecules move faster. So the water in the dish in the sun will evaporate faster!

Facts on Tap

Suppose you get caught outside in a rain shower on a hot, sunny day. Stay outside after the rain stops. The water in your clothes will evaporate, and you'll be all dry again soon!

The Water Cycle

CONDENSATION

PRECIPITATION

SNOW

RAIN

TRANSPIRATION

SURFACE RUNOFF

EVAPORATION

GROUNDWATER

GLOSSARY

atmosphere: the mix of gases that are all around Earth

comet: a space object made of ice and dust that has a long glowing tail when it passes close to the sun

crystal: a solid with a pattern of flat surfaces

meteorite: a piece of rock that falls to Earth from space

molecule: the smallest part of something

precipitation: rain, snow, sleet, or hail

puddle: a small pool of water

theory: an explanation based on facts that is generally accepted by scientists

transpiration: the giving off of water vapor through the leaves of plants

FOR MORE INFORMATION

Books

Paul, Miranda. *Water Is Water: A Book About the Water Cycle*. New York, NY: Roaring Brook Press, 2015.

Spilsbury, Louise. *What Is the Water Cycle?* New York, NY: Britannica Educational Publishing, 2013.

Stewart, Melissa. *Water*. Washington, DC: National Geographic, 2014.

Websites

Precipitation Education: The Water Cycle
pmm.nasa.gov/education/water-cycle
Read articles and watch videos to learn more about the water cycle.

The Water Cycle—USGS Water Science School
water.usgs.gov/edu/watercycle-kids-adv.html
Use this interactive website to take a virtual trip through the water cycle.

23

INDEX